TUG OF WAR

A Biblical Study that Journeys
Through Spiritual Warfare from
Creation to Crucifixion

Ashley Nichele Brown

TUG OF WAR

ISBN- 979-8-218-50340-6

www.AshleyNichele.com

Printed in the United States of America

2024

ACKNOWLEDGMENTS

Praise God, who is I AM, who is, was, and will always be my everything.

To my husband, Courtney, who saw and accepted every part of me. You are a testament to God's faithfulness and unconditional love.

To my good friend Lino, who shared the gospel on a Monday night in April 2015 and discipled me for years after.

To Tiffany, for the bible study invite…

Ephesians 4:14-15

So that we are no longer children [spiritually immature], tossed back and forth [like ships on a stormy sea] and carried about by every wind of [shifting] doctrine, by the cunning and trickery of [unscrupulous] men, by the deceitful scheming of people ready to do anything [for personal profit]. 15 But speaking the truth in love [in all things—both our speech and our lives expressing His truth], let us grow up in all things into Him [following His example] who is the Head—Christ.

Table of Contents

Chapter I

WARRING WITHIN

Each day, we face a choice to align with God or the world, to follow the spirit within us or our flesh. It's a beautiful privilege that our sovereign God grants us. Every morning, we wake to a war waging against our souls—an internal struggle for our lives. We have the freedom and power to choose Him or to choose us. The question remains: will we? Will we wake up to indulge our flesh or fulfill God's will? This is a decision we confront daily.

Salvation was a once-and-for-all decision by grace through faith, yet many who claim to be Christians do not live in accordance with Christian principles. As true believers and followers, our willingness to choose Him should supersede our desire to choose ourselves. Our lives are a series of choices, many of which are driven by a desire for fleshly satisfaction. If we were to take inventory of our lives at this moment, would we see God glorified or ourselves? These are questions we must ask ourselves as we prepare for battle. Take a moment to assess your current spiritual state; are you ready for the required pull?

We see the fruit of our decisions more clearly in the big moments. You know, when God's hand miraculously shows up and we run to tell everyone about it. Or when we are tempted, and we can boldly resist the enemy. Those are the moments we tend to boast about as Christians. We can easily identify what we are "not supposed to do," so we glorify ourselves as "good Christians" without recognizing that there is more to it than good or bad. What about the seemingly small moments that we are disobedient to? The list of do's and don'ts can be surface-level or overwhelming, but the key is simply recognizing that we are being pulled to and fro daily in a constant state of tug of war. A game that is not only to be won with strength but with strategy.

While I would like to insinuate that it has always been my keen ability to do what my spirit called me to all the time, that's not the truth. If I'm being honest, suppressing the desires of my flesh was a constant struggle. When Paul wrote in Romans that what he wants to do, he doesn't do, and what he doesn't want to do, he does... I felt that. I want to be able to say that I do what God wants me to do every waking day, but I don't. What I can say is, though, when it comes to tug of war, I am in a constant pull in a war that was already won for me. The good news tells us that we are conquerors in Jesus Christ through the power of the resurrection. Jesus getting up out of His grave three days after being crucified was foreshadowing what we would do in our lives spiritually.

This battle for all of us began in the garden. We usually start with Eve's conversation with the serpent, but I would like to propose the thought that it started before then. Let's take a step back and really dig into why she was susceptible to having a flesh versus spirit moment in the first place.

Genesis 1:26-27 Then God said, "Let Us make man in Our image, according to Our likeness; let them have dominion over the fish of the sea, over the birds of the air, and over the cattle, over all

*the earth and over every creeping thing
that creeps on the earth. So, God
created man in His own image; in the
image of God He created him; male
and female He created them.*

We must first understand that the spirit and
the flesh were not created simultaneously.
There is a disconnect between what the spirit
and heart want because they are two separate
parts. When God made man in chapter one,
He created the spirit of man. We were first
created in His image. He created our spiritual
personality and moral likeness after Himself.
The word "image" here translated from the
Hebrew is tselem (tseh'-lem). This word is
derived from a root meaning "to shade" or "a
phantom." The language is more figurative
than it is literal. Having this context gives us
more insight into God's desire for humanity.

To have Godlikeness is to have His Spirit and His dominion. This had nothing, yet, to do with arms and legs or a cute face but everything to do with the light inside of us. We were created for communion with The Creator. This is still God's intention for us. Apart from our relationship with Him, we are much like a fish out of water, gasping to be in the environment that is conducive to our existence. We immediately feel shame and separation when we are removed from His presence because we are outside our natural environment... in Him. We all possess God's likeness, but we don't all choose to walk in His likeness, and no one does all the time. The separate creation of flesh is written in Genesis chapter two to make it clear:

Genesis 2:5-7 Before any plant of the field was in the earth and before any herb of the field had grown. For the Lord God had not caused it to rain on the earth, and there was no man to till the ground; but a mist went up from the earth and watered the whole face of the ground. And the Lord God formed man of the dust of the ground, and breathed into his nostrils the breath of life, and man became a living being.

God spoke all of creation into being in just seven days. When He uttered the word, creation obeyed, including us, in spirit, on day six. When God observed that 'No man to till the ground' was present, He formed us from the dust in chapter two. This is where we become His handiwork. He fashioned our bodies and then breathed His breath into us.

Here is where we become a whole body and spirit with a soul. He made us in two parts on two different days. The first part is spirit, our true nature, our light and identity, which resembles Him. The second part is flesh, the physical being that we see. As we will see soon, the flesh is weak and susceptible to sin because of what it was created for. Our spirit-man was created for relationship and dominion with Him. Our flesh, on the other hand, was formed for service to Him. We see this in Genesis 2:15, where God took Adam and placed him in the garden to tend to it.

When we serve, a posture submission is required. To submit is to accept or yield to a superior force or the will or authority of another. With flesh being created to serve, it was literally formed to submit, making it more likely to be influenced by outside forces. This is why the flesh must be tamed and controlled, whereas our spirit-man has power and dominion in the "shade" of our God. Our soul, on the other hand, is hanging in the balance between the two. God graciously allowed us to choose which one we will serve, which is where most of us miss the mark. We have the power to say yes and walk in obedience and relationship with Our Creator, but we also have the option to say no and turn away to serve our flesh, creating a perpetual tug of war.

Like Eve, you may find yourself in a constant battle with your fickle flesh, but Jesus has already reclaimed your authority! The choice to retain or relinquish this authority is yours. We are in an unremitting struggle between our desires and what we know to be right. This continuous conflict between our polar natures leads to an ongoing identity crisis that plagues our generation. Paul addressed this in his letter to Rome:

Romans 7:14-25 AMP We know that the Law is spiritual, but I am a creature of the flesh [worldly, self-reliant—carnal and unspiritual], sold into slavery to sin [and serving under its control]. For I do not understand my own actions [I am baffled and bewildered by them]. I do not practice what I want to do, but I am doing the very thing I hate [and yielding to my human nature, my worldliness— my sinful capacity]. Now, if I habitually do what I do not want to do, I agree with the Law, confessing that it is good. So now it is no longer I who do it [the disobedient thing which I despise], but the sin [nature] which lives in me. For I know that nothing good lives in me, that is, in my flesh [my human nature, my worldliness—my sinful capacity]. For the willingness [to do good] is present in me, but the doing of good is not. For the good that I want to do, I do not do, but I practice the very evil that I do not want. But if I am doing the very thing I do not want to do, I am no longer the one doing it [that is, it is not me that acts], but the sin [nature] which lives in me. So I find it to be the law [of my inner self], that evil is present in me, the one who wants to do good. For I joyfully delight in the law of God in my inner self [with my new nature], but I see a different law and rule of action in the members of my body [in its

appetites and desires], waging war
against the law of my mind and
subduing me and making me a
prisoner of the law of sin which is within
my members. Wretched and miserable
man that I am! Who will [rescue me
and] set me free from this body of
death [this corrupt, mortal existence]?
Thanks be to God [for my deliverance]
through Jesus Christ our Lord! So then,
on the one hand I myself with my mind
serve the law of God, but on the other,
with my flesh [my human nature, my
worldliness, my sinful capacity—I serve]
the law of sin.

It is our duty to submit our flesh
to be in constant obedience to the
Spirit within us, just as Jesus did. Jesus
gave up His life, got up three days

later, and left the Holy Spirit so that we could be delivered from the exceedingly sinful nature of our flesh, which we must choose to die to daily. Adam and Eve relinquished their power that day in the garden, but we regained access through Jesus's life, crucifixion, resurrection, and the coming of the Holy Spirit. Once we accept His resurrecting power, we are continually transformed into the image of Christ, who died and was resurrected to impart His victory upon us. While the war began in that garden, it ended at the resurrection. When we decide to receive Jesus, the war ends within us, too.

Chapter II

THE PULL

Tug of war is a sport that pits two teams against each other in a test of strength. The teams pull on opposite ends of a rope, aiming to bring the rope a certain distance. Initially, this game was a contest for supremacy or authority over a space or thing. One would be challenged to a game of tug of war to show their strength and be granted a reward in their favor. Once the rope is over a certain distance, the team that pulls their opponent down wins. To win, you will attempt to pull the opposing team's marker across the line two out of three times.

What interests me most is that you'll notice each team gaining momentum during the game as they pull their opponent almost over that "certain distance." The closer they're pulled to the line, the more strength they seem to gain to pull away. It's like they use everything within them to win. It goes back and forth until someone finally gets their opposing team over the line! This is how life is for us. We're constantly swaying back and forth, gaining momentum, until eventually, one tug leads us into the arms of Jesus or the hand of the enemy. It is almost as if two voices are in our ears, one saying, "Come this way!" while the other pleads, "No, my way." But this is not just any old war. The trophy here is your soul. When we recognize the importance of this, we stop allowing our flesh to fight battles when Jesus has already won for us.

> *Ephesians 6:12 For we wrestle not against flesh and blood, but against principalities, against powers, against the rulers of the darkness of this world,*

against spiritual wickedness in high places.

If you are currently in a space where you're following the voice of God, and He has ultimately won the affections of your heart, but you struggle with walking it out in your daily life, there's hope for you. If your days are fully submitted to the Holy Spirit, but you desire to go deeper and hear His voice more intimately, there's hope for you. If you're feeling more like a surface-level Christian whose flesh gets fed more often than you'd like to admit, there is hope for you. Or, hey, if you're really like, "Yeah, my flesh has some big main character energy and is hard to tame," there is hope in the gospel for you, too.

Philippians 2:12b-13 Work out your own salvation with fear and trembling. For it is God which worketh in you both to will and to do of his good pleasure.

When you feel like there's little to no hope for your circumstance and you have given all you've got, don't forget that the blood of Jesus works on everything. He not only gives us the power to do what pleases Him, but He also gives us the will to do so. The Greek translation of "will" here is to "wish" or to "want," meaning all we want is what's pleasing to Him. That includes every stronghold you may be dealing with. So, ask yourself, "Who or what has supremacy or authority over my life at this very moment?" Are you identifying with who you were created to be? Or have your fleshly desires taken control?

I vividly remember the night I had a radical encounter with the Holy Spirit; I was in a constant state of tug of war, back and forth, back and forth. But I finally decided to give God supremacy and authority over my heart. God met me on a Monday in April 2015 in a living room full of strangers. Earlier that year, my cousin had consistently invited me to a young adult's bible study, but I pushed away her invites time after time. She had no idea that there was a spiritual war waged against my soul. I had stopped believing that there was a savior for me, but her constant invites were the beginning of the momentum I needed to pull back. In the four years leading up to that night, I was in a spiritual fight for my life.

At 18 years old, I got pregnant with twins, and I made the toughest decision I had ever had to make at that time. I decided to have an abortion. I thought the abortion would fix my "problem," but I had no idea that it would put me on a downward spiral of constant defeat. I was entering college on a full academic scholarship, which I would lose the following year. At the same time, I was trying to navigate my way around this vast void caused by grief, guilt, and shame. Those who represented Christianity at the time were heavily flawed, so I had no one to turn to for counsel, and the world was waiting for me with open arms. My disobedience had invited disaster into my life, and I didn't even try to pull back. I didn't think I could go to God because I felt so guilty, but I couldn't continue resisting the enemy alone.

So, let's fast forward to that Monday morning four years later. That day, I rode around my hometown in the passenger seat of my friend's car, feeling sorry for myself. After four years of living in darkness, it all came crashing down in an instant. My childhood friend was just killed in a freak accident while he was out evangelizing, and I can remember screaming and expressing how afraid I was. I didn't want to keep living a lifestyle that would destroy my soul. I was being pulled back and forth and lost all hope in myself, but the good news is, that's when God stepped in. You see, I had been trying to fight my own battles, not realizing that those battles were never mine to fight in the first place.

On one side of the rope, I struggled with traumatic nightmares, severe anxiety attacks, depression spells, chronic stomach ulcers, and immorality in every area of my lifestyle. I lacked identity, which is the root cause of most of our inequities. I was ending a destructive relationship attachment, planning to give in to a same-sex relationship, so lost that I would regularly see a psychic, seek various religions on the internet, smoke weed every day to sleep better, drink as much as I could, party multiple days a week, struggle with same-sex attraction, filled of grief and wickedness, and overall drifting further and further away from who I was at my core (a child of God, created in His image) but on the other side of that same rope was a bible study invitation…

Another text invite came through that Monday afternoon, and I finally said yes. I

would give this a shot before I
completely gave up on God. I
recognized that I couldn't do it without
help and needed something solid to fill
the voids of my life, but I knew that
what I was doing wasn't working. It was
out of my hands and had mercifully
fallen into His.

> Matthew 16:25 If *you try to hang on to*
> *your life, you will lose it. But if you give*
> *up your life for my sake, you will save it.*

My losing hope in myself led to radical
deliverance on a stranger's living room floor.
You see when I lost hope in myself, I allowed
God to step in and take control; I was set free
from the grief, identity confusion, and
brokenness that all stormed me like an

avalanche. He saved me from that storm and pulled on my rope.

Encountering Jesus was the most liberating encounter I have ever experienced! It was as if I was drowning with no hope of ever catching my breath again, so God breathed His breath into my nostrils. I mean, there He was... Just waiting for me to give the rope over to Him. He's merciful like that... Always waiting for us to draw near in the spirit, which permits His Spirit to draw nearer to us (James 4:8).

That Monday, I learned that things shift when we move out of the way. I learned that His grace is truly sufficient, and I need Him to help me walk this walk daily. In 2 Corinthians 12:9, Paul recounts a conversation he had with Jesus.

2 Corinthians 12:9 My grace is sufficient for you, for my power is made perfect in weakness.

The Greek word for "sufficient" is "arkeó," which means to assist, suffice, or to be enough. Grace has transformative power through the resurrection of Jesus Christ. Through grace, He gave us one of the greatest and most necessary gifts: salvation. This was Jesus's response to Paul asking Him to remove a thorn from his side that tormented Him. But He didn't remove the thorn. Instead, He reminded Paul that His grace is enough to sustain him, especially in his weaknesses.

We no longer have to feel hopeless or lose the war within. In our weakness, He is strong, and it is through Him, and Him alone, that we are made righteous. There is nothing we can do as mere humans to win this war other than to submit and surrender to Our Savior. Once I accepted that, He swept in and saved me from eternal doom. He saved me when I acknowledged that I was weak and hopeless and couldn't save myself. He can do the same for you; surrender is all you must do to receive that. You have control over every temptation and stronghold because He has given us the grace to resist and live for Him.

Give God supremacy, and He will give you freedom from bondage. My life is a testament to the hope and authority that believing in the Gospel of Jesus Christ gives us. Just because I handed over the ropes to my savior doesn't mean all these vices were not still on the other side, pulling me. They were, and if I'm being honest, some still are today. However, when I handed Him the ropes, I said no to everything that was unlike Him and yes to all of Him! With that new authority, we can speak to our flesh, "No, I will not entertain you. I will not give you power. You are not in control!" We can take contrary thoughts captive and pull for a life pleasing to God that leads others to Him.

Chapter III
CHOOSING SIDES

There is always a decision to be made. Whether you're hungry or getting dressed in the morning, your brain makes upward of 35,000 decisions each day, according to Eva Krockow, a lecturer at the University of Leicester in the United Kingdom. [1] That's like one decision every few seconds, and we live life hoping each one is right.

> Romans 8:7 *The mind governed by the flesh is hostile to God; it does not submit to God's law, nor can it do so.*

This verse encapsulates the struggle we all face: the conflict between our earthly, fleshly desires, spiritual growth, and obedience to God. A mind focused on worldly desires and sinful nature is in direct opposition to God's will and cannot align with Him. The word "hostile" originates from the Latin term "hostilis", meaning "enemy." The Greek translation is "echthros" which means "hated". A carnal mindset is an enemy of the Spirit of God. Every decision made that satisfies our carnal flesh goes against His Spirit, which aims to lead us toward righteousness and a deeper relationship with Him. Our choices can keep us afar or draw Him near, depending on which side we choose. It is not automatic. We still have to determine if God will be the Lord of our hearts or if we will choose a less worthy master, our flesh. But remember, choosing God's will brings freedom and empowerment, not bondage.

I can recall countless moments when I felt God tugging at my heart. At the time, I had no idea what that tug was, but looking back, I see that in my most challenging season, God was there. When I reached for Him, His hand was there waiting. For years, I chose to hate His way and love my own. I straddled the fence between God's intention and my feelings. "Feeling" is defined as a vague or irrational belief, emotional state, or reaction. This reminds me that feelings are not facts; as much as I would like to believe "my feelings are valid," they are deceptive. They are conjured up in our minds based on our experiences and beliefs. For most of those years of straddling, I allowed what my flesh felt to drive the choices I made. All those feelings led me into a pit. So, the next time you place your feelings on the throne, be reminded that God does not move based on your feelings. God moves based on your faith. Your feelings belong on the cross, where they can be crucified! Here is what the Bible tells us:

Matthew 16:24 If anyone wishes to follow Me [as My disciple], he must deny himself [set aside selfish interests] and take up his cross [expressing a willingness to endure whatever may come] and follow Me [believing in Me, conforming to My example in living and, if need be, suffering or perhaps dying because of faith in Me].

Galatians 5:24-25 Those who belong to Christ Jesus have nailed the passions and desires of their sinful nature to his cross and crucified them there. Since we live by the Spirit, let us follow the Spirit's leading in every part of our lives.

Ephesians 4:22-24 You were taught, with regard to your former way of life, to put off your old self, which is being corrupted by its deceitful desires; to be made new in the attitude of your minds; and to put on the new self, created to be like God in true righteousness and holiness.

Romans 6:6-7 For we know that our old self was crucified with him so that the body ruled by sin might be done away with, that we should no longer be slaves to sin— because anyone who has died has been set free from sin.

Simply put, Jesus instructs those who wish to follow Him to deny themselves of their deceitful desires. It is not easy, but Jesus's resurrection makes it possible. His resurrection was not only a historical event but a living reality that gives us hope and power. When Jesus raised himself from the dead and gave us authority over sin, it no longer controlled us. He graciously gave us the power to overcome those desires that come from our flesh. We have been graced to live as Christ lived.

> *1 John 3:6-9 Whoever abides in Him does not sin. Whoever sins has neither seen Him now known Him. Little children, let no one deceive you, He who practices righteousness is righteous, just as He is righteous.*

Abiding in Him means to "reside" or "stay" from the Greek word "menōn." I am reminded that it is not about whether we are strong enough to fight temptations and desires on our own. It is about whether we will choose to stay in His presence and nail those desires to the cross. If we can reside in Him and believe in His resurrecting power, those deceitful desires won't stand a chance. But are we willing to submit to His gracious power completely? If we are willing to endure a life that denies our desires, we will see Him. I say endure because denying the flesh of its satisfactions may cause temporary suffering. But it is better for the flesh to suffer for a moment than it is for the soul to be lost forever.

When we surrender to Jesus, He meets us where we are and sets us free from every stronghold that attempts to keep us in bondage. This does not mean He removes our thorns. It means He gave us our power back, so now, we can refuse to eat the fruit that the serpent offers. When I came face to face with Him, I chose His will over mine because I realized that the thorn in my flesh was not to be removed; it was to be surrendered! While we may have to deal with a thorn in our side, Jesus's pierced side reminds us that innocent blood was spilled for us. He took a spear to His side to show us that His grace is enough for the thorn in ours.

> Isaiah 53:5 But he was pierced for our rebellion, crushed for our sins. He was beaten so we could be whole. He was whipped so we could be healed.

> John 19:34 One of the soldiers, however, pierced his side with a spear, and immediately blood and water flowed out.

He modeled what it was like to endure, so when we choose Him, we choose that same sufficient grace—we choose life.

Chapter IV
DIG DEEPER

Pulling with the feet flat on the ground is impossible, a fault common to those not well-versed in the game. You would eventually be pulled in the opposite direction. To win the game of tug-of-war, you must learn to dig your feet deeply into the ground. Tug of War masters suggest cutting the heels or sides of both feet well into the ground. You can always differentiate those new to the game from those who have mastered it by how deep they are willing to dig in. This will require you to get dirt on your shoes and may even cause discomfort. It will require you to drive yourself into the foundation you are standing on to get a good grip on the ground. The key is to set yourself up to have strong resistance against your opponents. If you have ever played the game before and tried to keep your feet flat on the ground, you may have noticed yourself start to slip, and once you begin to slip, getting back into the fight seems impossible. You can never truly get enough grounding to pull yourself back, and eventually, you're pulled across the marker line. You have lost the game.

As you embark on this digging journey, be reminded that your deliverance is a ground-breaking event! This means that your very foundation must be shaken up and broken down to make room for your feet to get into position for warfare. God literally moved Heaven and Earth so that we could live a life of freedom in Him.

Our spiritual lives can feel "slippery" when we fail to truly dig in. We often settle for a surface-level relationship with God. We go to church, listen to sermons, read the verse of the day, play a little worship music in the car, pray one-sided prayers, and we call it a relationship with Christ. Yes, everyone has a starting point, but the issue comes when we get comfortable with our starting being enough. We have salvation and a routine that feels better than whatever chaos we participated in before, so we stick with it, and we never actually grow closer to Him or mature spiritually. The issue here is that without digging in, we make it easier for the enemy to pull us back where he wants us.

So, let me ask you this: if every relationship you have resembled your relationship with God, would you be considered a good friend? God doesn't just want to spend mornings or evenings with you. He's not just trying to catch up with you about your day. He doesn't want a low-maintenance friendship with you. He wants you to abide in Him. He wants to dwell in you. What and who we are wrestling with would love nothing more than for you to settle for the surface-level relationship that leaves you vulnerable to the pull.

If you don't truly dig in and continue digging in, the enemy of your soul knows it only takes one or two instances of warfare and resistance to start slipping back into what you were delivered from. While your starting point is to be cherished, I want to challenge you never to stop craving more of God. Never feel like you have arrived. Whether you are a new believer or a kingdom leader, you will never fully reach an ending destination because God is infinite. The more we arrive, the more

He continues to expose Himself, thus keeping us in a posture of perpetual reverence.

> *Luke 5:3-8 AMP He got into one of the boats, which was Simon's, and asked him to put out a little distance from the shore. And He sat down and began teaching the crowds from the boat. When He had finished speaking, He said to Simon, "Put out into the deep water and lower your nets for a catch [of fish]." Simon replied, "Master, we worked hard all night [to the point of exhaustion] and caught nothing [in our nets], but at Your word I will [do as you say and] lower the nets [again]." When they had done this, they caught a great number of fish, and their nets were [at the point of] breaking; so they signaled*

to their partners in the other boat to come and help them. And they came and filled both of the boats [with fish], so that they began to sink. But when Simon Peter saw this, he fell down at Jesus' knees, saying, "Go away from me, for I am a sinful man, O Lord!"

We see Jesus instructing the fishermen to "Put out into the deep water." In his response, Simon Peter explained that they had worked hard the entire night. This reminds me of us thinking we have done enough just because we are doing something. Like them working all night, we pray, we read our bible, and we go to church, but Jesus still says to go deeper. Showing us that our routines will only work for so long. When He commands us to go deeper, there's

something more He wants us to access.
The keys, as we see in the scripture
here, are to:

1) Start by following Jesus' instructions.
2) Be willing to lose control of your routine
and what you are accustomed to.
3) Be willing to reach out for help.

Once the disciples did this, their
obedience exposed them to a new
depth of God's power. The willingness
to do more than what they were used
to blessed them with an overflow
greater than they had ever
experienced. The deeper they went,
the more His character was exposed,
which led them to the final key:

4) Reverence for Jesus.

The Bible tells us that Simon Peter fell to his knees in reverence and that they were all completely astounded by the power of Jesus. God calls us to dig in for deeper devotion and reverence of Him & He will never run out of ways to amaze us.

Chapter V
A CHAMPION'S PULL

The problem with most people's pull is their unbelief. According to Hebrews 11:6, we must have faith to please God.

> *Hebrews 11:6 But without faith it is impossible to please him: for he that cometh to God must believe that he is, and that he is a rewarder of them that diligently seek him.*

The Bible also says in Ephesians 2:8 that we are saved by grace through faith. If faith is the channel through which His grace saves us, understand that there is no salvation nor pleasing God without believing God. Someone once asked me, "If all I have to do is believe Jesus died to be saved, then why does it matter what I do?" My answer to this question is a question. Do you believe in the entirety of Jesus' life, death, and resurrection?

The Gospel's main symbol in Western Christianity is the cross, but the cross isn't the whole story. If you believe in His life, you believe in His character, servitude, teachings, miracle-working power, and His way. If you believe in His death, you believe in His sacrifice, suffering, deliverance, and His mercy. And if you believe in His resurrection, you believe in His authority, redemption, and His power, which is the same power we now possess.

Our lives are reflective of what we believe in, and inconsistency is a form of disbelief. So don't think for a moment that you are not driven by your beliefs and convictions every single day. If you genuinely believe in something, it becomes your life. If it is not your life, there's a breach in your belief system.

For instance, Vegans are vegans because they have a deep conviction for animal rights or what they put into their bodies. Those who indulge in meat don't. A person who abstains from sex does so because they truly believe in being consecrated in that way. Those who indulge, again, don't. In the same way, when we truly believe in the totality of who Jesus is and what His life, death, and resurrection represent, we will live a life consistently expressing and honoring that belief. Those who lack belief in Him, don't. But the beautiful thing is that God even helps us with our unbelief.

"Help my unbelief" is a simple prayer in Mark, prayed by a father who asks Jesus to heal his son.

Mark 9:23-25 AMP Jesus said to him, "[You say to Me,] 'If You can?' All things

*are possible for the one who believes
and trusts [in Me]!" Immediately the
father of the boy cried out [with a
desperate, piercing cry], saying, "I do
believe; help [me overcome] my
unbelief.*

The Lord is willing and able to help you pull,
but you have to believe that for yourself.
The children of Israel's history tell a narrative
of tug-of-war. In the Bible, the children of
Israel are pulled back and forth from one side
of the rope to another as they grapple with
their faith. Swaying from complete devotion
to Him to idol worship and rebellion. In
Jeremiah 29:4-14, Jeremiah warns the
children of Isreal with the word from God,
who was about to allow them to be carried
away into captivity by Babylon.

Thus says the Lord of hosts, the God of Israel, to all who were carried away captive, whom I have caused to be carried away from Jerusalem to Babylon: Build houses and dwell in them; plant gardens and eat their fruit. Take wives and beget sons and daughters; and take wives for your sons and give your daughters to husbands, so that they may bear sons and daughters—that you may be increased there, and not diminished. And seek the peace of the city where I have caused you to be carried away captive, and pray to the Lord for it; for in its peace you will have peace. For thus says the Lord of hosts, the God of Israel: Do not let your prophets and diviners in your midst deceive you, nor listen to your dreams which you cause to be dreamed. They prophesy falsely to you in My name; I have not sent them, says the Lord. For thus says the Lord: After seventy years are completed at Babylon, I will visit you and perform My good word toward you and cause you to return to this place. For I know the thoughts that I think toward you, says the Lord, thoughts of peace and not of evil, to give you a future and a hope. Then you will call upon Me and go and pray to Me, and I will listen to you. And you will seek Me and find Me, when you search for Me with all your heart. You will find me, says the Lord, and I will bring you back from your captivity; I will gather you from all the nations and from all the places where I have driven you, says the Lord, and I will bring you

to the place from which I cause you to
be carried away captive.

Babylon is the city that we now call Iraq. Its name comes from *bav-il* or *bav-ilim*, which means "Gate of the Gods." Theologians call it a counterfeit of God's eternal city, Jerusalem. They worshipped false Gods and attempted to build a tower that would reach Heaven, referred to as the Tower of Babel in Genesis 11:4, but they were far away from God, living in pride and rebellion… The children of God lived the same way, contrary to what they were created for. So, God allowed Babylon to take His children captive. He delivered them into the hands of the thing they put before Him. They had given supremacy to what He had delivered them from time and time again. The side you give the most authority will consume you. But even though He allowed them to be consumed, He did not want them to stay there. In verses 5-9, God is still merciful and gives them grace to endure captivity. God assured them that when they seek Him, they will find Him, and He will listen when they call upon Him. He promises to deliver them from captivity. You have that same promise! God may have allowed you to be held captive by the lifestyle you placed before Him, but know that when you submit your heart back to Him, He will tug on the rope and rescue you!

When you feel you are losing yourself, don't forget His promises. In Lamentations, Jeremiah and the children of Israel are in bondage, living out the prophetic word God gave to Jeremiah. Jeremiah is lamenting, meaning mourning or crying out to God. He then remembers God's promise.

Lamentations 3:21-24 Yet I still dare to hope when I remember this: The faithful love of the LORD never ends! His mercies never cease. Great is his faithfulness; his mercies begin afresh each morning. I say to myself, "The LORD is my inheritance; therefore, I will hope in him!

Though God allows us to suffer, He has a plan that He is faithful to. His love is never-ending, and His mercies are new every single day. So, every day that we wake up, there's a new opportunity to receive His mercy.

We see the true power of having hope in God's power and faithfulness throughout the story of the Shunammite woman in 2 Kings 4:8-37. A woman from Shunem showed hospitality to the prophet Elisha by offering him meals and a room to stay whenever he passed through her city. Elisha was grateful for her servitude and prophesied that she would have a son despite her husband being old in age. The prophecy came true, but years later, her son died. She called for one of her servants to take her directly to the man of God, and she made it very clear to him that she would not return home without him, and only him, coming to see her son.

> *2 Kings 4:32-34 When Elisha arrived, the child was indeed dead, lying there on the prophet's bed. He went in alone and shut the door behind him and prayed to the Lord. Then he lay down on the child's body, placing his mouth on the child's mouth, his eyes on the child's eyes, and his hands on the*

*child's hands. And as he stretched out
on him, the child's body began to grow
warm again.*

We have all been that little boy,
just like the children of Israel. We were
lifeless and in need of a savior, and
Jesus placed His body in our place. We
were revived and brought back to life
as He stretched out on that cross. He
stretched out His arms where ours
should have gone. He put His mouth
and eyes where ours was supposed to
go. They pierced His hands in place of
where ours should have been pierced.
He took on all our shame, all our sins,
and every bit of wickedness inside of
us for us to be called righteous. He
gave up His life and was resurrected to
live forever, mirroring what we could

also do through faith. Once we surrender our lives to Him, we are raised to life with Him. So just because you are in a tomb now doesn't mean you have to stay there. You can come out of your lifelessness and live a new life in Jesus if you have enough faith to trust in the Champion.

If you genuinely believe in your heart that Jesus lived, died, and raised from the dead to give you power over falling into sin, you are saved from the hand of the enemy. When you believe in the authority Jesus gave you, you pull from a place of victory, knowing that God is the one pulling for you, and you don't have to fight those temptations or urges on your own.

That 18-year-old girl didn't know that God wanted to make a tug-of-war champion out of her. I had no idea of the full life I could have when led by Him. In my surrender, He healed me in a way that I could not have imagined. I pray my life reminds you that no matter how dark and filthy you may feel, no matter how broken and undone you think you are, He is strong in your weakest moments. God set me free almost 10 years ago, and He wants to do the same for you.

It's time to hand over the ropes.

Works Cited

Krockow, Eva. "How Many Decisions Do We
      Make Each Day?" Psychology Today, 27 September
      2018, https://www.psychologytoday.com/us
      /blog/stretching-theory/201809/how-many-
      decisions-do-we-make-each-day?amp. Accessed 29
      May 2023.

Author's Bio

Ashley Nichele Brown is a devoted believer and ordained pastor in Houston, TX. As a native of Lake Charles, LA, she enjoys good food and spending time with her family. She is the proud wife of Pastor Courtney Brown and the mother of a one-year-old baby boy.

She dedicates her life to exploring and sharing the profound truths of faith through discipleship and service. With a deep understanding of spiritual warfare and a heart for discipling others on their spiritual journeys, Ashley brings personal and powerful revelation to her writing.

In "Tug of War," Ashley combines biblical wisdom with personal insights to inspire readers to embrace God's will and find strength in surrender.

Made in the USA
Columbia, SC
11 October 2024

ea715848-f311-4831-bc46-e2a2cd850776R01